Other books by Stoecklein Publishing include *Seasons of the Steelhead, Photographing The West, The Cowboy Hat, Fly Fishing in Idaho, The American Quarter Horse, Cattle, The Cowboy Boot, Outhouses, Western Fences, Saddles of the West, California Missions, Dude Ranches of the American West, The Spur, The Western Buckle, Ranch Style, Cowgirls in Heaven, The Performance Horse, Cow Dogs, Lil' Buckaroos, The American Paint Horse, The Idaho Cowboy, Cowboy Gear, Don't Fence Me In, The Texas Cowboys, The Montana Cowboy, The Western Horse, Cowgirls, Spirit of the West,* and *The California Cowboy.*

Stoecklein Photography & Publishing
1730 Lear Lane, Unit A
Hailey, Idaho 83333
tel 208.788.4593 fax 208.788.4713 toll-free 800.727.5191
WWW.THESTOECKLEINCOLLECTION.COM

ILLUSTRATIONS   DON GILL
EDITOR   CARRIE LIGHTNER
DESIGN   ADRIENNE LEUGERS

Printed in China through
Four Colour Print Group, Louisville, Kentucky
Copyright © 2011 Stoecklein Publishing

ISBN 978-1-935269-21-2
UPC 6-80397-26921-3
Library of Congress Catalog number 2011933112

Introduction

COMMON SENSE AND A SENSE OF HUMOR

ARE THE SAME THING, MOVING AT DIFFERENT SPEEDS.

A SENSE OF HUMOR IS JUST COMMON SENSE DANCING.

~ Will James

Home to the cowboy is beyond the pavement, where the gravel road turns into dirt track. Cowboy trappings vary from East to West and North to South, but all have a few things in common: cold-jawed horses, dumb cows, and bull-headed cowboys. With this trio, there is always a calamity in waiting!

Growing up on a ranch, Don Gill was indoctrinated in the code of the West and has survived more than his share of wrecks. This book is a humorous look into the dos and don'ts of living the cowboy way that will bring a chuckle to the grizzled ol' hand as well as the saddle-sore greenhorn.

I would like to dedicate this book to my wife, Denise. She has put up with my crap for years, horses out in the middle of the night, sick calves on the kitchen floor, and deadlines that were put off to the last minute. Every successful cowboy knows that you need a wife with a good job in town.

A Handyman Jack, Fencin' Pliers And Baler Wire
Will Fix Anything On The Ranch

You Know You're On The Ranch When Next-Day Delivery Takes 5 Days

Always Remember Which Bottle You Drank From And Which Bottle You Spit In

A Cowboy Is Someone The Boss Hires To Annoy His Domestic Animals

Before Offering To Help The Neighbors' Brand,
Make Sure They Don't Have A Calf Table

Don't Take Your Best Girl Out Checkin' Heifers...She May Not
Find It To Be All That Romantic

Throwing $200 Of Hay At 30-Cent Cows May Seem A Little — Optimistic

Always Check Your Cinch Before Mounting

Always Use The Smallest Gauge Possible When Shooting Vermin In The Bunkhouse

Chewin' Tobacco Is Considered A Vegetable On Some Ranches

Just Like Ol' Charlie To Hog All The Shade

Always Ease 'Em Through The Gate To Get A Good Count

I Think The Boss Has Been Lowering His Standards To Meet His Expectations In Me

Never Drag 'Em To The Fire By One Hind Leg

One Of The First Skills A Cowdog & Ranch Horse Will Learn — Bar Broke

Did You Get A Good Count On 'Em?

A Lot Of Ranches Are Held Together By Low Wages, Long Hours, And Baler Twine

Pullin' Leather Beats Walking Everywhere

Never Hold The Nails In Your Mouth

Rabbit Fast, Turtle Slow

Directions To The Ranch — Turn At The Quick Stop And Follow The Beer Cans

Ah...Springtime On The Ranch...
When Your Size 9 Grows To A Size 15 In Three Steps

Don't Climb On The Gates

Never Cuss The Weather, It Will Get Worse

She Told Me She Wanted A Divorce For Our Anniversary...Damn!
I Didn't Want To Spend That Much

Never Leave The Neighbors' Jersey Bull Until The Next Morning,
He Might Cover 30 Of Your Finest Cows Overnight

Always Check The Trailer Latch Yourself

Don't Invite The Neighbors Over For The BBQ Until You Bury The Hide

Always Make Your Wire Gate Loose Enough For The Wife & Kids

Never Make Fun Of The Boss's Squeaky New Saddle,
It Might Be Your Old Bones

You Can Tell A Lot About A Ranch By The Quality Of The Horses

Sometimes Plan B Isn't So Pretty

Always Pick Up Your Haytwine

Don't Let Your Horse Tank Up On Water After A Hard Ride

If It Don't Kill You It's Funny

So Much For Being The Next Horse Whisperer

Never Offer Free Advice To Your Horseshoer

Sortin' Pairs Is Easier If It's Not Done At 30 MPH

Never Reach Into The Back Of A Ranch Truck

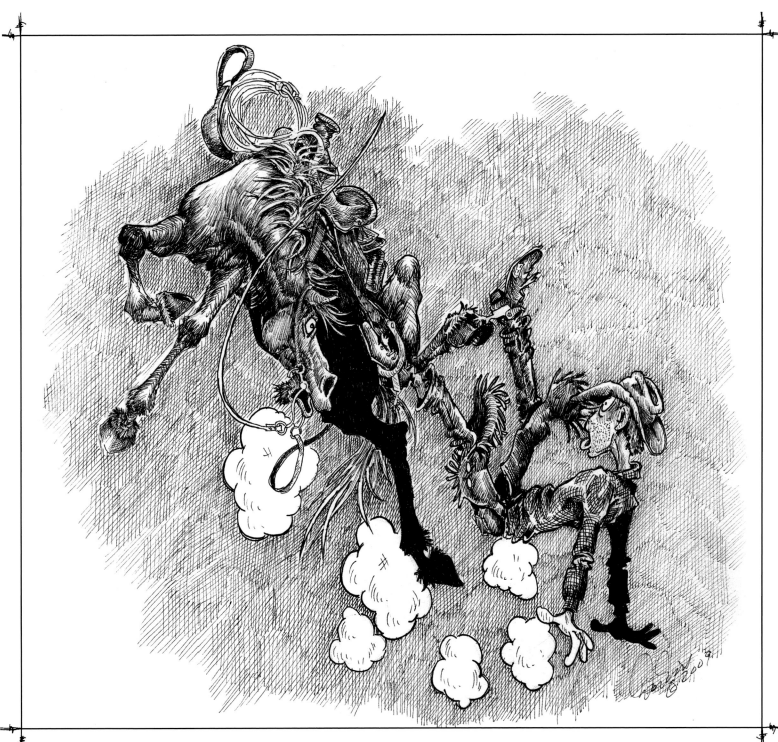

Don't Ride In Lace-Ups

The Boss May Not Like Your Dogs As Much As You Do

The Boss Has Kept Her 10 Years Longer Than He Should Have,
But She Does Know the Country

Never Run From Cows, It Teaches Them Bad Habits

Ol' Buck Has Been A Little Gassy, Doc

When There Is Frost On The Ground You May Want To Step Him Out First

Don't Bring 80 Feet Of Rope To The Branding When You Can Tangle Yourself Up With 30 Feet

It Would Help If The Cowboys Knew The Country As Well As The Cows

Always Drink Upstream

Never Run Your Horse Back To The Barn

The Highlight Of Every Ranch Dog's Life Is Chasing The Neighbor To The Front Gate

Always Shut The Gate Behind You

If Your Horse Ducks To The Left When You Dally, Pull The Other Rein

Drive West On A Dirt Road Until You Can't Get A Radio Station
And You're Almost To The Ranch

Never Tie To A Panel Or Gate

The New Guy's Afraid Of The Rattlesnakes
So We Put His Cell Phone On Vibrate

Never Tinkle On An Electric Fence

Always Take The Nose Tongs Out — Before — You Turn Her Loose

Even The Best Of Plans Have Drawbacks

Don't Break Out The Beer Before The Branding's Over

If You Can't Pee Off Of The Porch, Your Neighbors Are Too Close

*Anything More Than Yup And Nope And
You May Be Considered Too Much Of A Talker*

Always Try To Get Back Before The Noon Soap Is On

Never Assume You're Alone In The Outhouse

Heel Her Dammit, It Gets pretty Rough Up Ahead

*There Is A Reason To Be Concerned When The Boss Says
We're Gonna Take The Scenic Route Home*

Never Trust A Greenhorn To Hold The Rope Tight

They Always Look Smaller When You Pick The Fight

Always Undo The Back Cinch First

How's It Goin'...?

Sometimes Pairin' Up Isn't As Easy As It Sounds

Never Tie A Horse By His Bridle Reins

Don't Sit On The Outside Unless You Like Opening & Closing Gates